KU-523-075

This CBeebies Annual belongs to

_____

Published 2018.
Little Brother Books Limited, Ground Floor, 23 Southernhay East, Exeter, Devon EX1 1QL.
books@littlebrotherbooks.co.uk
The Little Brother Books Limited trademark, email and website are
the sole and exclusive properties of Little Brother Books Limited.

ISBN 978-1-912342-19-8

No part of this publication may be reproduced, stored in a retrieval system or transmitted in any form or by any means, electronic,
mechanical, photocopying, recording or otherwise, without the prior permission of Little Brother Books Limited.
All rights reserved. Printed in Poland, Europe.

A CIP catalogue for this book is available from the British Library.

Content created by Immediate Media:
Editor Andrea Turton Deputy Editor Jen Anstruther Senior Art Editor Maria Goodspeed Art Editor Stacy Roe
Senior Writer Daniella Wills Writer/Sub-Editor Becky Lord Joint Group Production Editors Carolyn Parris,
Marie-Louise Haig Deputy Group Production Editor Will Demetriou Production Editor Hannah Tibbetts
Deputy Production Editor Alastair Livesley Contributors Dan Morgan, Myfanwy Llywd-Williams.

Alphablocks © 2018 Alphablocks Ltd. All rights reserved. Alphablocks is a registered trademark of Alphablocks Ltd.
Andy's Prehistoric Adventures © BBC 2016. Andy's Safari Adventures © BBC 2018. Biggleton © BBC/CBeebies 2017. Bitz & Bob
© BBC & Boat Rocker Rights Inc. MMXVIII. Charlie and Lola logo ® and © Lauren Child 2005. Licensed by BBC Studios. Charlie and
Lola is produced by Tiger Aspect Productions. Text and illustrations copyright © Lauren Child/Tiger Aspect Productions Limited
2005-2008. Clangers © 2018 Coolabi Productions Limited, Smallfilms Limited and Peter Firmin. Get Well Soon © Kindle Entertainment
Ltd 2012. Illustrations by Plug-In Media. Gigglebiz © BBC 2015. Go Jetters © BBC 2014. Hey Duggee © Studio AKA Limited 2014.
Justin's House © BBC/CBeebies 2011. Kazoops © 2018 Cheeky Little Media Pty Ltd. My Pet and Me © BBC MMXV. Numberblocks
© 2018 Alphablocks Ltd. All rights reserved. OCTONAUTS™ OCTOPOD™ Meomi Design Inc. OCTONAUTS Copyright © 2018 Vampire
Squid Productions Ltd, a member of the Silvergate Media group of companies. All rights reserved. Peter Rabbit © Copyright Frederick
Warne & Co. Limited and Silvergate PPL Limited, 2018. Based on the works of Beatrix Potter. PETER RABBIT and BEATRIX POTTER are
trademarks of Frederick Warne & Co, a Penguin Group company. All rights reserved. Something Special © BBC 2004. Sarah & Duck
© Karrot Entertainment 2012. A Karrot Entertainment production for CBeebies. Licensed by BBC Studios. Swashbuckle © BBC/CBeebies
2014. Topsy and Tim TV series © Penguin Books Ltd and Darrall Macqueen 2018 Topsy & Tim™. Waffle The Wonder Dog © Darrall
Macqueen Limited 2018 Waffle The Wonder Dog™. Woolly and Tig © and TM Tattiemoon Ltd 2016. All Rights Reserved. CBeebies word
mark and logo are trademarks of the British Broadcasting Corporation and are used under licence. CBeebies logo © BBC 2002.

What's inside?

All about ME!

Say hello to your CBeebies House friends
and tell them all about YOU!

My **name** is:

I am

years old.

I'm B-e-n,
Ben! How do
you spell your
name?

Draw your
favourite food here.

I'm Cat.
My favourite
food is spaghetti.
What's yours?

I'm Rebecca.
I love swimming!
What's your
favourite hobby?

Hi, I'm Andy! How are you?

Draw **you and your family** here.

I'm Ryan. My CBeebies House friends are like a big happy family!

I'm Katy. Hello!

My family

I'm Dodge T. Dog, and this is Coogie!

7

Red

red

Colour the **red spots** on Mr Tumble's bow tie.

How many red spots did you colour?

8

Mr Tumble is choosing what to eat today.
Circle all the **red** food.

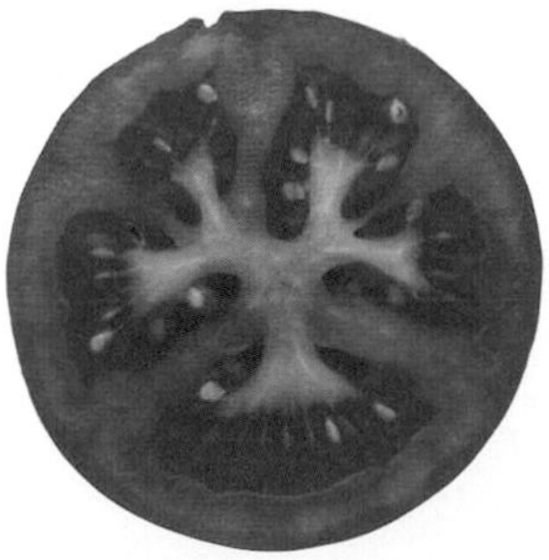

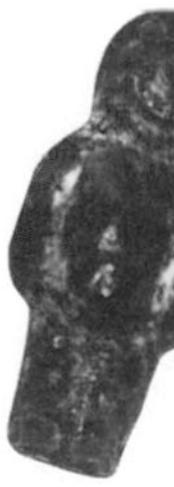

food

Give
Mr Tumble
a bright
red hat!

Duggee and the River Badge

1 "Hey, Duggee! What are you doing?" asked the Squirrels one morning. Duggee was going to deliver a parcel.

"Where to?" asked Norrie. Duggee pointed to his map. He was going to the end of a long river.

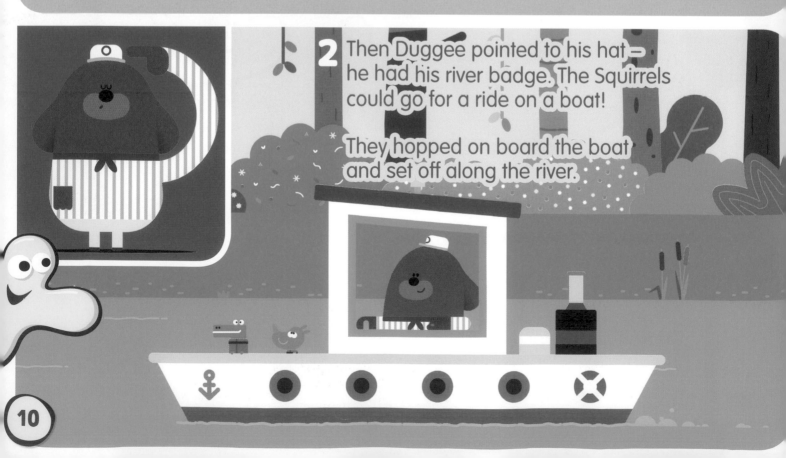

2 Then Duggee pointed to his hat — he had his river badge. The Squirrels could go for a ride on a boat!

They hopped on board the boat and set off along the river.

5 But then Happy spotted a waterfall and Duggee couldn't turn the boat in time...

...the boat...

...bounced...

...all the way...

...down.

GULP!

BOING!

BOING!

BOING!

SPLASH!

6 "That was fun!" giggled the Squirrels.

Then they noticed something strange. The boat was now full of colourful frogs.

"Woof-woof," said Duggee. They had arrived.

RIBBIT!

RIBBIT!

RIBBIT!

RIBBIT!

7 The Squirrels met a friendly rabbit on the land. "Follow me," he said. "She's been waiting for you."

Hey, man!

8 They went inside a cave and saw... Chew Chew the panda!

Hello, darlings!

9 The Squirrels gave Chew Chew her parcel. It was a big tin of biscuits!

10 "You can't have a cup of tea without biscuits," said Chew Chew. "And those greedy frogs ate my last ones."

Duggee and the Squirrels joined Chew Chew for tasty tea and biscuits. Their mission was complete!

Mmmm!

11 Haven't the Squirrels done well? They've earned their river badges!

12 There was just time for one more thing...

Duggee hug!

Our family

Say 'hello' to Topsy and Tim and their family!

This is Topsy and Tim's mummy. Her name is Joy.

This is Topsy and Tim's dad. His name is Brian.

Trace the letters.

Joy

Brian

I love riding my bike and going to the park with my twin sister Topsy!

I love to whizz about on my scooter!

Tim

Topsy

This is Topsy and Tim's home.
Draw a picture of **your home** here!

What colour is your front door?

Trace the letters.

My house

Bitz & Bob

Let's invent a way to save the day!

Engineer-o-Vision goggles

Tool belt pouch!

Colour Bitz!

Bitz makes amazing creations with anything she can find and brings epic adventures to life using her imagination!

It's time for a Bitz brain blitz!

Bitz uses her Engineer-o-Vision goggles to help her see answers to problems.

Write her name.

She is

years old.

Bob isn't just Bitz's little brother... he's her super robot sidekick!

Write his name.

Bob

He is

4

years old.

Colour Bob!

Torch

Hoo yeah! We're going on an adventure!

Juice box walkie-talkie!

Garden game

Race around the vegetable patch...
but don't let Mr McGregor catch you!

Start

1

2 Stop to raid some radishes! **Miss a go.**

3

Roll again. If you roll an even number, move ahead to space 14. If you roll an odd number, **move back to space 3.**

18 Finish **You made it!** Grab your vegetables and get back to the burrow!

We did it!

17

13 Don't let Mr McGregor catch you! **Stay here till you roll an odd number.**

16 Mr Tod is lurking nearby... **lie low and miss a turn.**

14 Collect some tasty carrots. **Roll again!**

15

Why, hello there...

HOW TO PLAY:
This is a game for 2-5 players.

1 Find some small things, such as buttons, to use as counters and put them at the start.

2 Take turns to throw a dice and move around the board.

3 The first player to reach the finish has escaped Mr McGregor... and is the winner!

Peter Rabbit

4 Watch out for Mr McGregor's cat! **Move back 1 space.**

6 Save Benjamin from a falling plant pot! **Hop ahead 1 space.**

Thanks for your help!

5

7

8 Spot one of Mr Rabbit's secret tunnels. **Follow the path to the signpost.**

12

10

9

11 Lily has a clever plan! **Move forward 1 space.**

RUN, RABBIT, RUN! Throw again.

19

Animals ahoy!

Colour in Gem, Captain Captain, Cook, Line and their new animal friends!

Hi there, m'hearties!

 Now try Gem's Swashbuckle salute! Let me see you all marching...  Hand on your heart...

Ahoy, little frog!

Jet Pad trails

Help the Go Jetters get back to Jet Pad.
Watch out for the Grimbots!

Jokes! Jokes! Jokes!

Have a giggle at Dodge's jokes, then rate them using the Fun-O-Meter!

Q. What happens when it rains cats and dogs?

A. You might step in a poodle!

Funny rating

Q. What did the cat have after she ate a ball of wool?

A. Mittens!

Funny rating

Q. Why did the cat put the letter M in the freezer?

A. To turn 'ice' into 'mice'!

Funny rating

Q. What do you call a dog detective?

A. Sherlock Bones!

Funny rating

I'd be great as Detective Dodge!

24

Q. What do you call a dog magician?

A. Abraca-labrador!

Funny rating

Q. Which cat delivers presents at Christmas?

A. Santa Claws!

Funny rating

Q. How does a dog stop her favourite TV show?

A. She presses the paws button!

Funny rating

Q. Why are cats such good piano players?

A. Because they're so mewsical!

Funny rating

Fun-O-Meter

1 2 3 4 5

100% not funny! Woof!

Fur balls are funnier than that joke!

I've got the kitty giggles!

That joke was barking mad! Ha ha ha!

Paw-sitively hilarious!

Q. Which dogs like taking baths?

A. Shampoodles!

Funny rating

La-la-la! Ha-ha-ha!

25

colour

Alphablocks

f g h t j

o p q r

w x y z

n o p q r s t u v w x y z

27

Hot and cold

Let's find out which animals live where it's hot and cold.

Colour a yellow sun to keep the animals warm

Koalas...
live in Australia. They can spend up to 18 hours a day asleep. Zzzzzz!

Meerkats...
can be found in Africa. They live in big groups. Everyone takes turns getting food and looking out for predators.

Orangutans...
live on Asian islands. They spend nearly all their lives in trees!

Draw a chilly blue snowflake here.

Harp seals...
have thick blubber to stay warm in cold water.

apanese macaque monkeys...
take baths in hot springs to stay warm in freezing weather!

Mountain goats...
have long coats to protect them from cold mountain winds.

These monkeys wash their food before they eat it.

Polar bears...
have black skin under their fur to absorb the sun's warm rays.

29

Let's count

Help the Numberblocks count their things by writing the numbers in the boxes.

tree

socks

hats

presents

stars

Breakfast buddies

Grab your pencils and create some funny breakfast people!

Rise and shine, it's funny food time!

Your funny food could look like this:

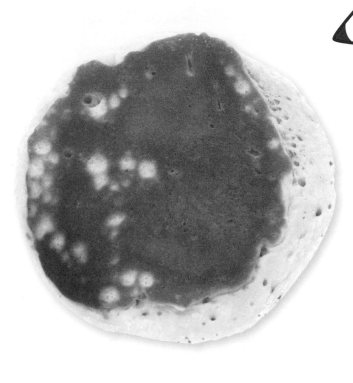

This is Barry. He is egg-cellent!

Baby dinos

Colour this prehistoric bunch with your pencils!

Dinosaurs hatched from eggs. Can you spot 5 dinosaur eggs in the picture?

Did you know?
Scientists don't know what colour dinosaurs really were because only their fossils remain!

Illustrated by Ian Cunliffe.

Justin Town

Help Justin find a way through the
Justin Town maze to his house.

Start

Count the
ducks.

NEWSAGENT

JUSTIN
IS
LOST!

DUCK
LAKE

Count the jellies.

JELLY FIELDS

Count the sheep.

Justin's House

Can you spot Little Monster?

Finish

37

Dino doodles

Use your imagination to fill the dinosaur kingdom with colourful dinosaurs.

What sound do you think the dinosaurs made, Jimmy Jones?

OINK!

Kazoops!

Invent your own dinosaurs or follow these steps to draw a T-Rex...

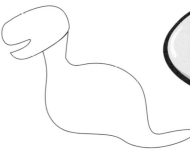

1. Begin with a head shape like this.

2. Add a body.

3. Draw the legs and little arms.

4. Finally add teeth, eyes and nostrils!

Meeting friends

Follow the trail and do the tasks as you meet the residents of Biggleton!

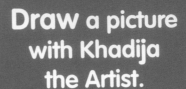

Draw a picture with Khadija the Artist.

START

Special delivery!

sunflower seeds

IMPORTANT

Sign for a parcel from Ava the Postie!

Please sign for your parcel here!

40

Write your name here.

Do a **Biggle** wiggle with Momo the Athlete!

Biggleton

I've been busy baking!

Decorate a cupcake with Aleem the Baker.

How many test tubes?

Colour the test tubes for Professor Millie.

FINISH

Which was your favourite Biggleton job?

Space snack

Have a blast with this rocket sandwich!

> Cut your sandwich into a triangle for the rocket.

> I nibbled a cucumber moon and a cheese star!

> Decorate your rocket with radish, cucumber and carrot.

> We made cheese and pepper rocket boosters!

> Carrot sticks make great flames!

42

Origami

Origami is a craft where you make amazing things by folding paper. Try making this origami Dodge!

1 Fold a piece of paper like this and **snip** off the extra piece so you have a triangle.

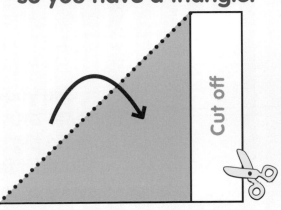

Cut off

2 Fold the points down on the long side for ears so it looks like this.

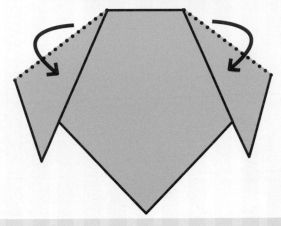

3 Fold up one side from the bottom.

4 Draw on a nose, tongue and eyes. Lastly, **scribble** on brown fur.

This is grrr-eat!

43

Pet care

Find out how to care for these lovely animals!

Hi, I'm Rory! I love pets!

Grooming

Pets with fur need to be groomed. This means brushing them so their fur stays clean.

Use your finger to brush this guinea pig's fur. Would it feel spiky or soft?

Bathing and cleaning

Dogs need to have baths with special shampoo. Their teeth also need to be brushed!

Draw over the dotty line, then colour this puppy's toothbrush!

Exercise and play

Pets need lots of space to run around and play. Bigger pets, like dogs, need to be taken for regular walks!

Colour some toys for this kitten to play with!

Healthy diet

Pets need to be fed a healthy diet. It's important to make sure they have fresh food and water every day.

Draw something healthy and yummy for this rabbit to munch on!

I'm Ferne! What's your favourite pet?

Story-ing!

Design a book cover for Lola, then finish Charlie's story.

Lola says, I **read** to our **pumpkin** because plants LIKE being talked to.

Here are some ideas for your pumpkin cover...

A pumpkin story by
Write your name.

A pumpkin story by
Write your name.

A pumpkin story by
Write your name.

A pumpkin story by
Write your name.

Write these words in the story:

ball

glass

prince

It was time for the Princess to go to the ....

She put on her .... slippers and stepped into the

beautiful carriage. She had an extremely fun time

Circle a word.   singing   dancing   eating

all night with the ....

Then the clock struck 12. The Princess hurried home in

her carriage, just before it turned back into a pumpkin.

And the pumpkin lived happily ever after with the

Circle a word.   carrot.   potato.   mushroom.

The end.

Footy fun

Draw and colour to help
Keith Fitt be a football star!

I've been playing football for over 20 years!

Finish the big boot.

Colour a bright football for Keith!

Let's warm up!
Try these moves.

Gigglebiz

1 Stretch out those legs.

Time to move!

2 Balance on 1 leg.

Wobble!

Champion!

3 Kick the air to pretend to score!

4 Lift your arms and give a big cheer.

GOAL!

You did it!

49

Handy art!

Simply draw around your hand to create these hand-y creatures.

Choose a creature and have a go here.

a camel

an elephant

a jellyfish

a chicken

Great job!
Give me
a high 5!

Try again here!

You're good at this!

Do you like my paw-some picture?

Odd one out

Scribble over the odd one out in each group.

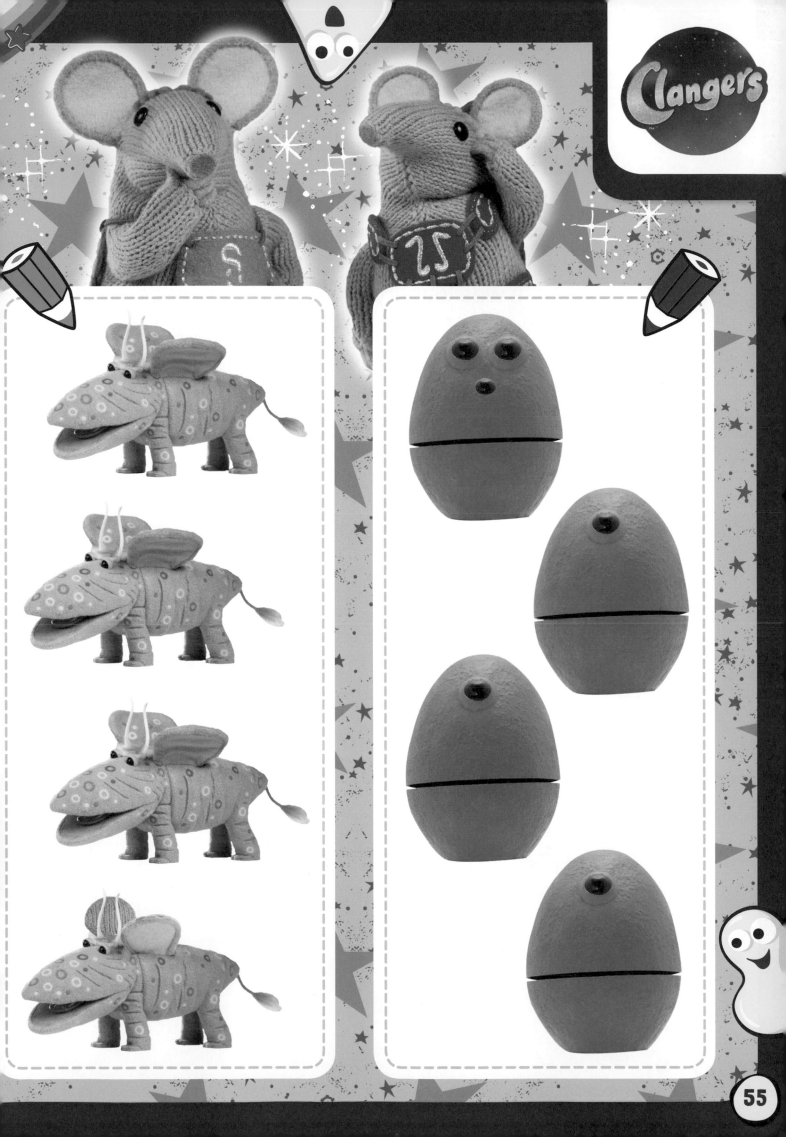

Training Day

Read all about Waffle's silly smelly sock training day!

Urgh, what a pong!

It was laundry day and Simon needed to wash his smelly socks. "Ew!" giggled Evie. "They're really pongy, Dad!" cried Doug. But Waffle loved Simon's smelly socks. **"Mmm, socks!"** he sniffed, and quickly hid a sock in the best hiding place... Jess's handbag!

Later, Jess, Evie, Doug and Gramps took Waffle to a puppy training class. "Remember, Waffle, no talking!" they whispered to him.

The teacher taught all the dogs how to sit and roll over, but Waffle was in a silly mood and wouldn't listen. Then Jess found Simon's sock in her handbag and Waffle got very excited! "Maybe Waffle will behave if we offer him the smelly sock as a treat," said Doug. What a good idea! Waffle sat and rolled over, just like the other dogs! **"Smelly sock!"** giggled Waffle.

Calm down, Waffle!

MIAOW!

"Shhh! No talking, Waffle!" whispered Evie and Doug. **"What about a miaow?"** Waffle thought to himself. **"Miaowww!"** he yowled, loudly. Uh-oh... all the dogs in the puppy training class thought there was a cat in the room and started running about and barking! **"Hehe!"** Waffle chuckled.

Hey! My sock!

Hehehe!

Back at home, Simon had been looking everywhere for his missing sock. "It was in my bag!" Jess told him. "How did it get there?" Simon asked. "How do you think?" Evie and Doug laughed, looking over at Waffle.

Waffle waved at them with his paw. He just loved Simon's smelly socks!

The end

57

Octonauts HQ

Get busy with the Octonauts!

parrotfish

Dashi has typed her name.
Write over the letters.

Dashi

Colour the letters that spell out your name.
Then press the buttons on the keyboard.

q w e r t y u i o p
a s d f g h j k l
z x c v b n m Enter

surgeonfish

We've got lots to do. We need your help!

Aye, aye, Captain!

Press the Octo-Alert button when you find it!

Incy Wincy Woolly

Sing the song with Tig then colour Woolly's boots.

Incy Wincy Woolly climbed up the water spout. Down came the rain and washed poor Woolly out!

Sing with us!

How do you think Woolly felt **when he climbed to the top of the spout?**

puzzled

happy

How do you think Woolly felt **when he was washed away?**

grumpy

excited

Out came the sunshine,
and dried up all the rain.
So **Incy Wincy Woolly**
climbed up the spout again!

63

Unicorns

Use your pencils to colour this magical picture!

Great colouring!

Illustrated by Cathy Hughes.

Time for school!

Topsy and Tim love school!
Can you help them with their schoolwork?

Look at the pictures and **circle** the correct spellings.

 **bag** or **bug**

 **van** or **vin**

 **tid** or **ted**

hut or **hat**

School is fun and our teacher is lovely!

Have a go at these sums.

1 + 2 = [ ]   2 + 2 = [ ]

It's art time! **Match** the numbers
to the colours to finish the picture.

1
2
3
4

Brilliant
colouring!

2 + 3 = ☐   3 + 3 = ☐

Leaf hunt

Colour a leaf each time you spot a difference!

1 2 3 4 5

Tick the boxes when you find these leaves in the pictures.
Psst: they're in the same place in both pictures!

6 7 8 9 10

Let's make!

Try these simple makes using cardboard tubes.

Use your penguin as a pen pot!

Animals

Paint cardboard tubes or cover in coloured tissue paper.

Cut out and **stick** on shapes like penguin feet or a fox's tail.

Draw on faces. **Push** down the top of the tube to make ears.

What will you name your knightly castle?

Castle

Paint cardboard tubes and **tape** them together to make a castle.

Roll card into cones for roofs.

Rocket

Roll a cone out of card and **stick** it on the end of a painted tube.

Cut out paper flames and stick them on the other end.

Look at that rocket go!

WHOOSH!

Houses

Cover a tube with bright wrapping paper.

Pop a cupcake case on top to make the roof.

Draw windows and doors.

Who lives in a tiny house like this?

71

Let's read a story together.

Little Red Riding Hood

Shout out the big words in the story!

A little girl lived by a **wood.**

She always wore a bright red **hood.**

She went to see her gran one **day,**

but met a wolf along the **way!**

"Where are you going?" he asked with a **grin.**

"To see my gran," said Red. "I hope she's **in!"**

So the little girl carried on **walking.**

She had no more time for **talking.**

Wolf ran off as fast as he **could.**

He knew a shortcut through the **wood...**

He reached the house before young **Red,**

locked up Gran and jumped in **bed!**

Illustrated by Helen Rowe.

72

She'll never guess I'm not her dear old Gran!

Knock! Knock!

Dressed in poor old Gran's night **clothes,**
Wolf pulled the sheets up to his **nose.**
At last Red reached the house and **knocked.**
"Come in," called Wolf. "The door's **unlocked!**"

"Why, Grandmama," Red said with **worry.**
"Your teeth are big and you look... **furry!**"
"The better to eat you with!" Wolf **cried.**
He growled at Red, mouth opened **wide!**

But Red was brave and she was **strong.**
She'd guessed it was Wolf all **along!**
She chased him out, as quick as can **be,**
and unlocked Gran in time for **tea!**

The end

Sweet dreams

Even when you're asleep, your brain is busy making dreams. Draw what the gang are dreaming about.

Zzz...

Snore!

Snore!

Answers

Pages 8-9

There are **7** spots to colour on Mr Tumble's bow tie.

The red things are:

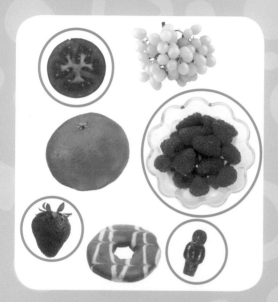

You're a star!

Pages 30-31

1 **2** **3** **4** **5**

tree   socks   hats   presents   stars

Pages 34-35

Pages 36-37

There are **4** ducks.

There are **5** jellies.

There are **3** sheep.

Pages 46-47

It was time for the Princess to go to the ... **ball** ... .

She put on her **glass** slippers and stepped into the beautiful carriage. She had an extremely fun time

Circle a word. singing   dancing   eating

all night with the **prince** .

Then the clock struck 12. The Princess hurried home in her carriage, just before it turned back into a pumpkin.

And the pumpkin lived happily ever after with the

Circle a word. carrot.   potato.   mushroom.

The end.

Pages 66-67

The correct spellings are:		The answers to the sums are:
	bag	1 + 2 = 3
	van	2 + 2 = 4
	ted	2 + 3 = 5
	hat	3 + 3 = 6

Pages 54-55

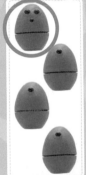

Pages 68-69

Well done if you spotted all 10 differences!